D0053864

MOTHER AND CHILD

ever ancient, ever new

CHRISTINE GRANGER

PARACLETE PRESS
BREWSTER, MASSACHUSETTS

2018 First Printing

Mother and Child: Ever Ancient, Ever New

Published in Canada by Novalis Publishing Inc., 10 Lower Spadina Avenue, Suite 400, Toronto, Ontario, M5V 2Z2.

ISBN 978-1-64060-149-9

Library of Congress Cataloging-in-Publication Data

Names: Granger, Christine, author.
Title: Mother and child : ever ancient, ever new / Christine Granger.
Description: Brewster, MA : Paraclete Press, Inc., 2018.
Identifiers: LCCN 2018027097 | ISBN 9781640601499 (hardcover)
Subjects: LCSH: Motherhood—Religious aspects—Christianity. | Mary, Blessed Virgin, Saint.
Classification: LCC BV4529.18 .G733 2018 | DDC 242/.6431—dc23
LC record available at https://lccn.loc.gov/2018027097

10 9 8 7 6 5 4 3 2 1

Published by Paraclete Press
Brewster, Massachusetts
www.paracletepress.com

Printed in the United States of America

Contents

To you, Mother of the human family
and of the nations,
we confidently entrust the whole of humanity,
with its hopes and fears.
Do not let it lack the light of true wisdom.
Guide its steps in the ways of peace.
Enable all to meet Christ,
the Way and the Truth and the Life.

Pope John Paul II

I: Motherhood

A mother's service is nearest, readiest and surest:
nearest because it is most natural,
readiest because it is most loving and
surest because it is truest.

Julian of Norwich

Nine months before I was born there was a woman who loved me deeply. She did not know what I was going to be like, but she loved me because she carried me in her womb. And when she gave me birth, she took me in her arms because her love was not just beginning. She conceived it along with me.

Oscar Romero

MP
IC
XC

We two form a multitude.

Ovid

There is no more witness to the mystery of the Word made flesh than a baby's naked body. I remember with sensory clarity sitting with one of my babies on my lap and running my hand over the incredibly pure smoothness of the bare back and thinking that any mother holding her child thus must have at least an echo of what it is like to be Mary: that in touching the particular created matter, flesh of our child, we are touching the Incarnation.

Madeleine L'Engle

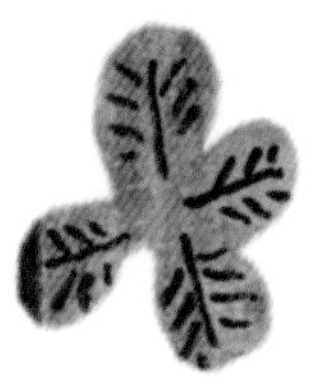

II: The Motherhood of Mary

IC
XC

I drew him close to me with affection and love;
picked him up and held him close to my cheek;
I bent down to him and fed him.

Hosea 11:4

In the depths of darkness
she gave birth to light.
In the depths of silence
she brought forth the Word.

Byzantine prayer

Sleep, sleep, my Holy One!
My flesh, my Lord! – what name? I do not know
A name that seemeth not too high or low,
Too far from me or heaven;
My Jesus, *that* is best! That word be given
By the majestic angel whose command
Was softly as a man's beseeching said,
When I and all the earth appeared to stand
In the great overflow
of light celestial from wings and head
Sleep, sleep, my saving one!

Elizabeth Barrett Browning

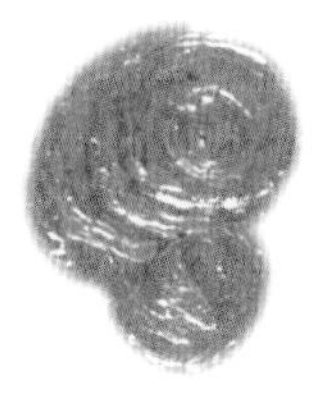

Enough for Him, whom cherubim
worship night and day,
Breastful of milk,
and a mangerful of hay;
Enough for Him, Whom angels fall before,
The ox and ass and camel which adore.

Angels and archangels may have gathered there,
Cherubim and seraphim thronged the air;
But His mother only, in her maiden bliss,
Worshipped the beloved with a kiss.

Christina Rossetti

The Christ-child lay on Mary's heart
His hair was like a fire.
(O weary, weary is the world,
But here the world's desire.)

The Christ-child stood at Mary's knee,
His hair was like a crown.
And all the flowers looked up at Him,
And all the stars looked down.

G. K. Chesterton

Tender one, hail!
Hail mother of love!
You bore for the world
a child sent from Heaven
whom the Spirit of God
inspired.

Glorify the Father,
the Spirit
and the Son,
whom the Spirit of God inspired.

Hildegard of Bingen

М
МБ
IC
XC
89

His smooth arms reach
making a harmonious
symmetrical arch
to hold up the world.

Krucor Ha Noregats
(Armenian, 11th c.)

. . . voices chime in heaven
and the whole earth
marvels at Mary
beloved beyond measure

Hildegard of Bingen

Mary is symbolic of life, birth, and growth.
At the same time, Mary is an intercessory figure.
That's her mission, that's why she was born.
I believe that Mary would want us to be life-saving
beings, and nurturers.

Robert Lax

Again and again
she comes into our lives,
into the life of the world
to bring joy and peace.
To lead us back to God.

Mother Teresa

The rose is a mystery, where is it found?
Is it anything true? Does it grow upon ground?
It was made of earth's mould but it went
from men's eyes
And its place is a secret and shut in the skies.
In the gardens of God, in the daylight divine
Find me a place by thee, mother of mine.

Is Mary the rose then? Mary the tree?
But the blossom, the blossom there, who can it be? –
Who can her rose be? It could be but one:
Christ Jesus our Lord, her God and her son.
In the gardens of God, in the daylight divine
Shew me thy son, mother, mother of mine.

Gerard Manley Hopkins

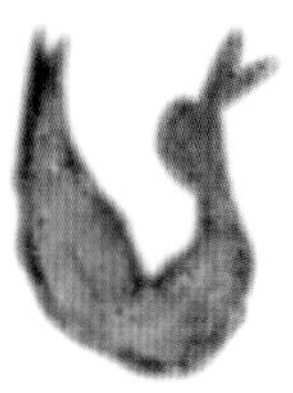

III: Prayers

And we pray to him
for the love of the
sweet mother who
bore him,
and the help
we have of her,
it is of his goodness.

Julian of Norwich

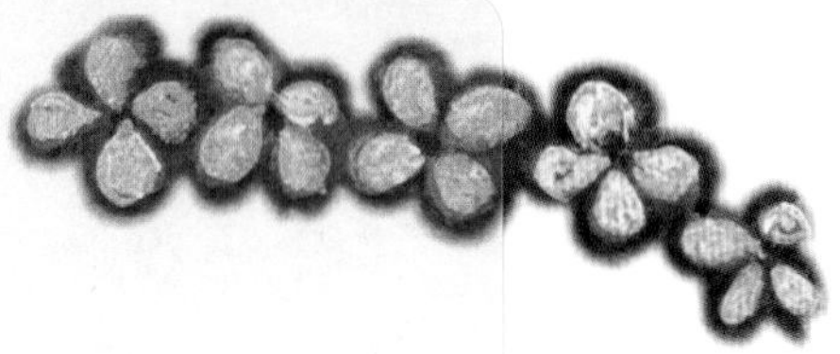

Mirror of justice,
preserve in us
the love of divine grace
so that living humbly and happily
in obedience to our Christian calling,
we may always enjoy
the Lord's friendship
and your motherly consolation.

Pope John XXIII

Mother of Christ
Light in all darkness
Shelter him
Our flame of love

And in our times
of dread and nightmare
let him be our dream
of comfort.

And in our times
of physical pain and suffering
let him be our healer.

And in our times
of separation from God
and from one another
let him be our communion.

Fr. William Hart McNichols

MP
MБ
IC
XC

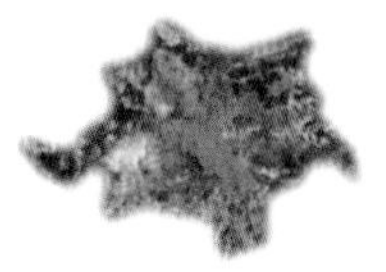

Lady, Queen of Heaven,
pray me into solitude and silence and unity,
that all my ways may be immaculate to God.
Let me be content with
whatever darkness surrounds me,
finding Him always by me, in His Mercy.

Thomas Merton

My hope is all in you
Bright Eden
in your kind mercy, Mother.
In you I trust,
O holy strength of all the saints
immaculate and full of grace

Taras Shevchenko

Mary, you plead for us all,
Lift up your voice and carry
our souls above on the wings
of your call.

Hildegard of Bingen

And a sword will pierce your own soul too.

Luke 2:35

There abideth on her brow
The ended pang of knowledge,
  the which now;
Is calm assured.
Since first her task began,
She hath known all.

Dante Gabriel Rossetti

Father, you give your daughters strength
A double portion to sustain us through
the loneliness of loss and leaving,
the child, the man, forced from our breast.
Help us to turn and trust you for the rest.

Rowena Edlin-White

At morn – at noon –
at twilight dim –
Maria! Thou hast heard my hymn!
In joy and woe – in good and ill –
Mother of God, be with me still!

Edgar Allen Poe

For the child who comes again
Who each morning
makes the light sing
For the child who comes again
Who will take us with him to-morrow
I greet you, Mary.

André Dumont

Lily herself, she bore the one
Fair Lily; sweeter, whiter, far
Than she or others are:
The Sun of Righteousness her Son,
She was His morning star.

Christ's mirror she of grace and love,
Of beauty and of life and death:
By hope and love and faith
Transfigured to His likeness, "Dove,
Spouse, Sister, Mother," Jesus saith.

Christina Rossetti

MP
IC
XC

Lady, thy goodness,
thy magnificence,
thy virtue,
and thy great humility
surpass all science and
all utterance.

Geoffrey Chaucer

Mary is our mother, the cause of our joy. Being a mother, I have never had difficulty in talking with Mary and feeling close to her.

Mother Teresa

MP
IC
XC

Mother of Christ
Mother of Christ
What shall I ask of thee
I do not wish for the
wealth of the earth
For the joys that fade and flee.

But Mother of Christ
Mother of Christ
This do I long to see
The bliss untold which
thy arms enfold
The treasure upon thy knee.

Anonymous

I sing of a maiden
That is matchless,
King of all kings
For her son she chose.

He came as still
where his mother was
as dew in April
that falls on the grass.

He came as still
to his mother's bower
As dew in April
That falls on the flower.

He came as still
Where his mother lay
As dew in April
That falls on the spray.

Mother and maiden
There was never one but she;
Well may such a lady
God's mother be.

Anonymous

A new thing dawns today
for which the round earth seeks to grow more wide.
What is a thornbush now: God feels his way
into a virgin's womb. I am the ray
thrown by her inwardness, which is your guide.

Rainer Maria Rilke

In the incarnation
God reveals himself
without concealment.

Dietrich Bonhoeffer

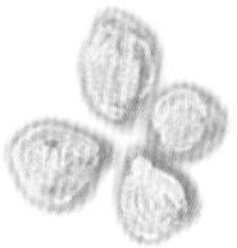

The Word did not appear out of the skies
as a powerful superman.
The Word became flesh,
conceived by the Holy Spirit as a tiny human being,
invisible, hardly formed,
yet totally prepared for growth.
He came out of the womb of this woman
and lived in a deep relationship with her.
He needed her presence, her love, her warmth,
the nourishment that flowed from her breasts.
He became part of the history of the human race.
The Word who became flesh
needed this double preparation,
one very hidden, the other very visible.

Jean Vanier

A mother came to mould
Those limbs like ours which are
What must make our daystar
Much dearer to mankind;
Whose glory bare would blind
Or less would win man's mind.
Through her we may see him
Made sweeter, not made dim,
And her hand leaves his light
Sifted to suit our sight.

Gerard Manley Hopkins

Imagining Mary in words and pictures
has always been one of the most powerful ways
of imagining the Church,
and so of imagining ourselves freshly.
May we help others to imagine
and to encounter the child of Mary
as we go to our business of discipleship.

Rowan William

Sources

p. 5: Pope John Paul II, "Our Lady of the Millennium, Mother of the Redeemer" Marian Prayer, 1999.

p. 9: Julian of Norwich, *Showings*. E. Colledge and J. Walsh, trans. New York: Paulist Press, 1978, p. 297. Oscar Romero, *The Violence of Love*. Farmington, PA: Plough Publishing House, 1998, p. 71.

p. 11: Madeleine L'Engle and C.F. Chase, *Glimpses of Grace: Daily Thoughts and Reflections*. New York: Harper Collins, 1998.

p. 17: Elizabeth Barrett Browning, "The Virgin Mary to the Child Jesus," 1838.

p. 19: Christina Rossetti, "In the Bleak Mid-winter," 1872.

p. 21: G. K. Chesterton, "A Christmas Carol," 1900.

p. 23: Barbara Newman, *Symphonia: A Critical Edition of the Symphonia Armonie Celestium Revelationum.* New York: Cornell University Press, 1995, p. 111.

p. 25: Ibid., p. 129.

p. 27: Steve Georgiou, *The Way of the Dreamcatcher: Spirit Lessons with Robert Lax.* Ottawa: Novalis, 2002, p. 221. *He's Put the Whole World in Her Hands: Quotations of Mother Teresa of Calcutta, India*. Compiled and edited by Dan Paulos. Roselle, IL: Roman Inc., 1989, p. 60.

p. 29: Gerard Manley Hopkins, "Rosa Mystica," 1875.

p. 33: Julian of Norwich, *Showings*. E. Colledge and J. Walsh, trans. New York: Paulist Press, 1978, p. 185.

p. 35: *Days of Devotion: Daily Meditations from the Good Shepherd, Pope John XXIII.* New York: Viking Penguin, 1967, p. 114.

p. 39: Thomas Merton, *Dialogues with Silence: Prayers and Drawings.* Edited by Jonathan Montaldo, San Francisco: Harper San Francisco, 2001, p. 135.

p. 41: Taras Shevchenko, "Maria," 1859. Translated by Christine Granger. Newman, *Symphonia*, p. 119.

p. 43: Dante Gabriel Rossetti, "A Virgin and Child, by Hans Memmeling; in the Academy of Bruges," *Collected Poetry and Prose*, ed. Jerome McGann (New Haven, CT: Yale University Press, 2003), pp. 344–45; *Dancing on Mountains: An Anthology of Women's Spiritual Writings.* Edited by Kathy Keay and Rowena Edlin-White. London: HarperCollins, 1996, p. 88.

p. 45: Edgar Allan Poe, "Catholic Hymn," 1845. André Dumont, from Hervé Aubin, *The Lord Is with Thee.* Notre Dame du Cap: Novalis, 1988.

p. 47: Christina Rossetti, "Herself a Rose Who Bore the Rose," ca. 1877.

p. 49: Geoffrey Chaucer, "The Prioress' Prologue," in *The Canterbury Tales.* Mother Teresa, *In My Own Words.* Compiled by L. Gonzales-Balado. New York: Gramercy Books, 1996, p. 59.

p. 55: Rainer Maria Rilke, "Annunciation to the Shepherds from Above," in *Rilke Poems*, Trans: J. B. Leishman and Stephen Spender. New York: Everyman Pocket Library Series, Knopf, 1996. Dietrich Bonhoeffer, *Christ the Centre.* New York: Harper & Row, 1978.

p. 57: Jean Vanier, *Drawn into the Mystery of Jesus through the Gospel of John.* Ottawa, ON: Novalis, 2004, p. 29.

p. 59: Gerard Manley Hopkins, "The Blessed Virgin Compared to the Air We Breathe," 1918.

p. 63: Rowan Williams, *Ponder These Things: Praying with the Icons of the Virgin.* Norwich, UK: Canterbury Press, 2002, p. 74.

Every effort has been made to locate sources for previously published material. Any oversights will be corrected in future editions of this book.

The Paintings

I have been painting Mary since the early 1980s, and continue to paint her almost daily. "Of Mary there is never enough," says St. Bernard, and I agree. My starting point is the Ukrainian and Byzantine icon tradition, but I consider all art, past and present, as my heritage and inspiration.

I see Mary as a gentle and gracious woman, fully in tune with God's will. She is always with her Son; she points to him, she leads us to him. I like to think of my work as an echo of Gabriel's words: "Hail Mary, full of grace, the Lord is with thee…." Each painting is a joyful reaffirmation of the mystery of the incarnation.

The artist's technique

Although I have used various media, including wax and egg tempura, I now use acrylic colours and acrylic gold. The technique of layering that I employ is widely used in iconography. Many layers or coats are applied to achieve what looks like a single colour. I like to build up textures, patterns and borders by applying paint in thick lines and layers. I love to work with reds, oranges, yellows and golds, colours usually associated with fire, light and the divine.

The mother and child image goes back to prehistoric times. Perhaps that is why both believers and non-believers respond to it. Artistically, the two figures are treated as a single unit. The painting is put into the Christian context by the initials near the figures: Mary, the Mother of God and Jesus Christ.

Christine Granger